# Parent Guide

## AGE 3–5

### Jim Fitzsimmons and Rhona Whiteford

Illustrated by Sascha Lipscomb

## Contents

**Hodder Children's Books**

**The only home learning programme supported by the NCPTA**

# Introduction

Children learn more, and at a greater speed, during the pre-school years than at any other time in their lives. It is a time of considerable personal, social, emotional and physical development, from gaining an understanding of the world and how to interact with it to developing language and communication skills.

As a parent, you can play an important part in your child's education by showing interest and encouragement. This book is designed to offer advice about how you can support your child's natural inclination to explore and learn. It includes lists of practical, purposeful activities that you can introduce to your child, information on groups and support services for parents and children, and advice about playgroups, nurseries and preparing your child for school. It also includes checklists of things you might expect your child to be doing at certain ages. These are intended only as a guide to what you should be encouraging your child to do. It is important to remember that all children are individuals who learn at their own pace.

These are some general guidelines for helping your child to develop and learn:

- Talk to and listen to your child as much as possible. Also, sing and read together as much as possible.
- Encourage regular contact with other children and adults.
- Assist your child to learn things for herself. Offer lots of encouragement and help when needed.
- Consider your child's own interests when organising activities, and remember that enjoyment is the key to success when learning new skills.
- Plan activities and outings together.
- Take advantage of everyday opportunities to involve your child in a variety of activities such as baking or gardening.
- Encourage curiosity about the world and try to develop your child's skills of observation and discussion. Set an example by your own interest and enthusiasm.
- Visit a variety of places: a town, a city, a forest, a mountain, the seaside, a zoo, a farm, a station, an airport, a hospital, the shops, a theatre, a railway station, a swimming pool, a nursery.

# Developing a positive attitude

**If your child enjoys doing activities with you she will often be learning at the same time. The way in which you react to your child's efforts will have a great influence upon her attitude towards the activity on future occasions. Enjoyment and success will foster a positive attitude whatever the activity, and praise for work that is well done will help boost your child's confidence.**

❑ Encourage your child to listen to what people are saying. This is especially important when following instructions or if there are safety considerations.

❑ Encourage your child to ask questions and to seek help if she is unsure of what to do.

❑ Stress the need for co-operation and sharing.

❑ Try to develop a positive attitude to learning in your child, so that she sees learning situations as a challenge, not a threat.

❑ Work with your child to solve problems and overcome difficulties. If she says, 'I can't do it...', show that help is always at hand to face the challenge and find the solution.

❑ When your child is struggling with an activity, it is important to praise the things she can do to boost her confidence. Progress at her rate, and increase the difficulty of a task very gradually.

❑ It's better not to force your child to do something she doesn't want to do. Work at new things together but give the minimum help needed and point out afterwards how little you helped. Always praise what she has achieved and build on that in gradual stages.

❑ Whatever activities you do together, make sure you are both relaxed and have enough time. Make sure that you are unlikely to be interrupted. Remember that it is the quality of the time spent together that counts, not the quantity.

❑ Provide a variety of short activities and ensure effective learning by approaching any activities as an enjoyable challenge rather than a chore.

Always finish on a high note and give your child plenty of opportunity to repeat and reinforce what she has done.

❑ When your child is successful, help her to see her success as preparation for the next step forward and to look upon every situation as a learning opportunity. Try to foster eagerness and anticipation for what is to come next.

❑ If your child is not successful, rather than saying something is wrong, you could say, 'You were almost right. Let's try again together.' Point out where she got things right and show that the solution is within sight.

❑ Foster good concentration by following instructions together. Your child will practise looking and listening carefully as you follow a recipe, play a board game or read books together.

❑ Always involve your child if she shows an interest in things you are doing. Allow a bit more time than you would take on your own and go more slowly. Explain things and show patiently what you want the child to do.

❑ Develop an enquiring mind by encouraging your child to ask questions of the 'Why?', 'How?', 'Where?' variety. Answer her questions as fully and in as much detail as she can handle.

❑ Encourage good observation by pointing things out as you go for walks or visits. Encourage your child to collect things, and always involve her if you need to search for information about the things you find.

❑ Always encourage your child to complete tasks. To this end it is important that you do not overload her and expect too much. The tasks should not be too difficult if you want to avoid boredom and frustration.

❑ Reward good behaviour and achievement. Lots of praise reinforces and encourages positive attitudes. You could keep a record of particular milestones in the form of a chart, so your child can see her progress for herself.

# Physical development

As the parent of a pre-school child, you will never cease to be amazed by his boundless energy. The constant movement and exploration of his surroundings are essential to both his physical and his mental development. Through tackling his environment and handling the objects around him, he gains control, mobility, confidence and knowledge. You can help him by introducing stimulating and challenging environments together with lots of encouragement.

## LARGE MOVEMENTS (whole body)

All the following experiences are helpful:

❏ Playing games such as football, catch, hide-and-seek and statues

❏ Going to the park to swing, slide, push, pull, climb, balance, jump and land

❏ Going to the swimming pool; swimming lessons

❏ Going to gymnastics, riding or ballet lessons

❏ Learning to ride a tricycle or bicycle

Try these activities, too:

❏ Throwing and catching a ball or beanbag

❏ Aiming at a target

❏ Aiming a football between home-made goalposts

❏ Hoopscotch - hopping from hoop to hoop; try using sets of coloured hoops and hopping to one colour only

❏ Negotiating a simple obstacle course, on foot or on a tricycle

❏ Jumping over a skipping rope with feet together, first with the rope swinging, and then with the rope turning in a circle

❏ Sliding down and crawling up a smooth, flat plank

❏ Jumping, rolling and stretching on floor cushions and old mattresses

## CHECKLIST

| Age 3 | Age 4 | Age 5 |
|---|---|---|
| Can he: | Can he: | Can he: |
| ❏ walk forwards, backwards and sideways? | ❏ stand, walk and run on tiptoes? | ❏ walk confidently along a narrow line? |
| ❏ walk on tiptoes? | ❏ stand on one foot for a few seconds? | ❏ skip confidently? |
| ❏ stand on one foot for about one second? | ❏ hop on his preferred foot? | ❏ run on the balls of his feet? |
| ❏ climb nursery apparatus confidently? | ❏ throw, catch, bounce and kick a ball with confidence? | ❏ play ball games with some success? |
| ❏ ride a tricycle using the pedals and steer it round large objects? | ❏ use a bat and ball? | ❏ move rhythmically to music? |
| ❏ throw a ball from chest height and catch a ball with arms extended? | ❏ climb ladders and trees? | ❏ swing, slide and climb on large apparatus? |
| ❏ kick a ball? | | |
| ❏ move round obstacles while running, and manoeuvre push-along and pull-along toys round them? | | |

- Walking on paint-can stilts - take 2 old paint cans and attach a long cord 'handle' to each one
- Newspaper cricket - make a bat from a rolled-up newspaper and a ball from a screwed-up single sheet of paper
- Foot painting - soak a flat sponge in an old washing-up bowl of water-based paint; your child paints the sole of his foot by pressing it on the sponge, then walks over a large sheet of paper, making a footprint with each step

- Finger painting
- Making collages using lots of different materials
- Making pipe cleaner people
- Making models from clay
- Threading large wooden beads on to a lace, or small wooden beads on to thin cord
- Doing jigsaw puzzles
- Building with construction toys

## SMALL MOVEMENTS

All the following experiences are helpful:

- Using a fork and spoon or a knife and fork together
- Pouring juice from a jug into a cup (practise with water over a large bowl)
- Unscrewing the top from a bottle or jar
- Fastening large buttons on clothes

Try these activities, too:

- Practising holding a pencil correctly
- Tracing a picture
- Drawing round a shape
- Colouring pictures, trying to colour within the lines

## CHECKLIST

| **Age 3** | **Age 4** | **Age 5** |
|---|---|---|
| Can he: | Can he: | Can he: |
| ❑ build a tower of 9 cubes or more? | ❑ build a tower of 10 cubes or more? | ❑ thread a large needle independently and sew some stitches? |
| ❑ thread large wooden beads on to a lace? | ❑ thread small beads to make necklaces (with some adult help)? | ❑ copy a square, and, later, a triangle? |
| ❑ hold and control a pencil? | ❑ copy a cross? | ❑ form a few letters? |
| ❑ copy a circle? | ❑ draw a very simple house? | ❑ draw a house with a roof, a door, windows and a chimney? |
| ❑ cut paper with scissors? | ❑ match the colours red, yellow, blue and green and say their names? | ❑ colour pictures within the lines? |
| ❑ match the colours red and yellow and say their names? | ❑ pick up tiny objects between thumb and first finger? | ❑ name 4 or more colours and match 10 colours? |
| | ❑ cut paper accurately with scissors? | |

# Social behaviour and play

The pre-school child is actively exploring her world, beginning to understand her environment and forming relationships with other people.

## SOCIAL BEHAVIOUR

Your child needs to learn:

- to be independent
- to solve problems
- to differentiate between right and wrong
- to work in a group
- to show sensitivity to others' feelings

You can help her by encouraging her to:

- ❑ dress herself
- ❑ tidy away her own clothes and toys
- ❑ feed and wash herself
- ❑ help with jobs around the house
- ❑ take turns
- ❑ learn about personal safety*
- ❑ be positive about personal skills and qualities ('I am good at...', 'I enjoy...')
- ❑ share her own toys with friends
- ❑ have friends round to play and visit friends' homes
- ❑ go to playgroup/nursery
- ❑ learn good manners
- ❑ meet a variety of people and visit places with you
- ❑ learn to make choices

---

## CHECKLIST

| Age 3 | Age 4 | Age 5 |
|---|---|---|
| Does she: | Does she: | Does she: |
| ❑ eat with fork and spoon? | ❑ use a fork and spoon capably? | ❑ use a knife and fork capably? |
| ❑ wash her own hands (but usually need help to dry them)? | ❑ wash and dry her hands and brush her teeth independently? | ❑ wash and dry her face and hands independently? |
| ❑ pull her own pants and trousers up and down (but need help with buttons)? | ❑ dress and undress independently except for laces and buttons on the back of a garment? | ❑ dress and undress independently? |
| ❑ stay dry through the night? | ❑ behave more independently? | ❑ behave in a controlled, sensible and self-reliant way? |
| ❑ behave affectionately and openly? | ❑ argue and quarrel if she doesn't get her own way? | ❑ appreciate the need for tidiness? |
| ❑ like to help adults with housework/ gardening? | ❑ show a sense of humour? | ❑ take part in quite complicated floor games? |
| ❑ help to keep the environment tidy? | ❑ enjoy make-believe play and dressing up? | ❑ enjoy both large-scale and small-scale construction toys? |
| ❑ begin to understand the difference between present and past? | ❑ enjoy the companionship of other children? | ❑ choose some of her own friends? |
| ❑ begin to accept the necessity of having to wait for certain things such as treats and special outings? | ❑ appreciate the need to ask for things from others rather than simply to snatch them? | ❑ understand the need for rules and co-operative behaviour? |
| ❑ enjoy make-believe play with imaginary people and objects? | ❑ understand the need to take turns? | ❑ show a developed sense of humour? |
| ❑ participate in make-believe play with other children? | ❑ understand the difference between past, present and future? | ❑ begin to understand the meaning of clock-time in relation to her own daily activity? (not yet able to tell the time) |
| ❑ enjoy playing with bricks, construction toys, toy trains, dolls and prams either with others or independently? | ❑ display concern for younger children and those in distress? | ❑ behave protectively towards younger children and pets? |
| ❑ understand the need to share toys with others? | | ❑ show sympathy towards friends? |

# PLAY

Children have a natural urge to play. It is their need to explore the world and the objects around them that fuels this, and in the process they learn the majority of their early skills. The importance of play should never be underestimated.

The quality of the learning that takes place during your child's periods of play will be dependent on the adults around her. It is you who provide the play materials whilst offering guidance and encouragement. However, you also need to know when to step back and allow her to make her own discoveries.

Play takes many different forms, but they all stimulate the imagination, give a sense of achievement and help develop powers of observation, concentration and communication. The following activities provide good learning opportunities as well as being fun:

## Messy play

Provide plastic aprons to protect clothes, and use an area where your child does not need to worry unduly about mess. Teach your child to limit the mess and encourage her to help with the tidying up afterwards.

## Play with water

❑ Play in the bath or sink, or use a large washing-up bowl. In the summer, set up an inflatable paddling pool.

❑ Provide a variety of containers of different sizes for pouring.

❑ Try floating different objects in water. How many of them sink?

❑ Try adding sugar, salt and powder paint to small containers of water to see what happens.

❑ Add washing-up liquid to water and make bubbles.

REMEMBER SAFETY AT ALL TIMES.

## Play with sand

❑ Use a sandpit, an old washing-up bowl or a babybath, or fill an old tyre.

❑ Buy silver sand, not builder's sand.

❑ Provide lots of different equipment: jelly moulds, pastry cutters, old scales for weighing, paper bags, spoons, plastic cups and other containers, wooden spoons.

Children particularly enjoy pretending to cook or bake with sand.

❑ Mix sand and water.

❑ Make patterns and pictures in the sand using a finger or a stick.

❑ Cover sand kept outside to prevent it from getting dirty or wet. Be especially careful about not letting pets play in it.

❑ Clean sand by rinsing it in a solution of sterilising fluid.

## Imaginative play

Young children take great delight in their own imagination and learn many new skills in the process. Through dressing up and pretending to be another person or creature, children can begin to imagine how it feels to be someone else. Playing with dolls, dolls' houses, soft toys, puppets, cars, garages and cardboard boxes stimulates talk and can provide an outlet for a range of feelings. When imaginative play includes other children (social play), ideas about right and wrong behaviour are developed.

❑ Keep dressing-up clothes in a large box or laundry basket. Clothes could include: hats, bags, old jewellery, scarves, aprons, shoes (not with high heels). Also include tablecloths, sheets and towels.

❑ Toddlers like having a den to play and hide in. A den can easily be made by draping a sheet or curtain over a table or chairs.

## Explorative and experimental play

❑ Let your child explore the properties of playdough (recipe on page 19) as she squeezes and squashes it.

❑ Use clay to make models.

❑ When cooking, let your child help with the stirring and mixing, cutting and decorating.

❑ Try various recipes with your child, to see what happens when you mix and cook ingredients.

❑ Try growing things together.

## Constructive play

Provide plenty of opportunities for your child to play with a variety of bricks, construction kits, empty boxes and other junk materials.

---

*Feeling happy, feeling safe* by Michelle Elliot (Hodder) may be helpful here.

# Activities to help language development

We use language in lots of different ways, for lots of different purposes. Through language we can:

- explain
- wonder
- state
- amuse
- warn
- question
- greet
- excite
- delight
- entertain
- answer
- command
- calm
- direct
- describe

Be aware of your own use of language and notice whether your child uses it in a variety of ways. The following activities will help your child's language skills:

❏ Spend lots of time talking with your child.

❏ Listen carefully to each other.

❏ Give running commentaries and ask lots of questions.

❏ Sing rhymes and songs with lots of repetition, and encourage your child to listen carefully to the words.

❏ As you look at and read books, talk about the pictures and, as your child gets older, ask questions such as 'What can you see?', 'Who is this?', 'What is he doing?', 'Where is the...?'

❏ Stress key words in the things that you say.

❏ Listen to stories on radio, television and tape.

❏ Encourage your child to have opinions - talk about poems, stories, songs and rhymes. What do you enjoy about them? Why? Teach him to listen to and respect other people's opinions.

❏ Play games - table games need lots of social conversation! Play snap and matching games, do jigsaws and teach a child who has started to read to play games involving making up words from letters.

## SPEAKING

Communication skills can be developed by playing and talking games such as:

❏ **Snap** Play this in the usual way, but encourage your child to say what the cards have in common.

❏ **Remember, remember** Help your child to develop his imagination and memory. Start off with 'Mrs Briggs has a baseball cap...' Your child repeats the line and adds another item of clothing. Take turns to build up a list of the clothes Mrs Briggs is wearing.

❏ **Imagine** Start by saying, 'Imagine I was small... I could ride on the toy train...' Take turns with your child to say what you could do, wear, eat and see...

❏ **What is wrong?** Draw pictures of people in strange situations or with something odd about them. Your child has to say what is wrong and why.

❏ **Feely bag** Put several objects in a bag. Your child puts his hand in and tries to identify an object. Ask your child to describe the object before he brings it out.

❏ **Daily diary** Keep a record or diary of trips or outings to help your child remember special events.

❏ **Add a line** Start off a story and encourage your child to add a little more. Take turns until the story is completed.

❏ **Right order** Divide an everyday action such as getting dressed into 4 or 5 steps. Draw these on cards for your child to sort into the right order and describe.

❏ **Puppet show** Using puppets, ask your child to tell a familiar story.

## LISTENING

Understanding is the result of good listening skills. Develop your child's listening skills with the following simple activities:

❏ **Listen and draw** Your child draws a picture as you give instructions for him to follow.

❏ **Find it** Ask your child to find something you describe.

❏ **Question, question** Take turns to ask questions such as 'Why do we need cars?' Encourage your child to think of as many reasons as possible.

❏ **Which way now?** Make a giant map together and put in lots of landmarks such as the park, the shops, the library, the church, the cinema. Your child has to follow your instructions to move a toy car around the map.

❏ **Give us a clue** Cut pictures from magazines and mount them on cards. You hold the cards and you give the clues. Your child has to guess what each picture shows.

❑ **Guess the words** When singing action songs or rhymes, miss out the action word to see if your child can guess the word from the action.

❑ **Treasure hunt** Hide an object or a treat and give your child clues to help find the hidden 'treasure'.

❑ **Obstacle course** Set up a simple obstacle course in the garden or the house. Your child has to follow instructions such as 'Go over the chair, under the mat and round the table.' This gives practice in understanding position words such as 'over','under' and 'round'.

The following computer software may be helpful:

❑ Pre-school language programs on standard computers and CD-ROM

❑ Interactive stories on CD-ROM

❑ Any computer game which encourages discussion

---

## CHECKLIST

### Age 3
Does he:

❑ speak with varied loudness and pitch?

❑ have a wide vocabulary that is understandable to those both inside and outside the family?

❑ have a basic grasp of grammar?

❑ pronounce some letter sounds correctly?

❑ give his full name and, sometimes, his age?

❑ use personal pronouns ('I', 'you', 'he', 'she', 'we', 'they', 'me', 'him', 'her', 'us', 'them') correctly?

❑ use plurals and most prepositions ('above', 'below', 'inside', 'on' etc) correctly?

❑ ask lots of questions of the 'What?', 'Why?', 'Where?' 'Who?' variety?

❑ know several nursery rhymes?

❑ love to listen to stories - particularly familiar ones?

❑ recite numbers up to 10 or more but usually only appreciate the value of those up to 3?

❑ hold simple conversations and briefly describe present and past activities?

❑ hold long conversations with himself - often in make-believe activities?

### Age 4
Does he:

❑ speak in a way which is easy to understand and grammatically correct?

❑ pronounce more letter sounds correctly?

❑ give his full name, address and, often, his age?

❑ ask 'Why?', 'How?' and 'When?' questions constantly?

❑ give accurate descriptions of recent experiences?

❑ recite numbers up to 20 but usually only appreciate the value of numbers up to 5?

❑ know several nursery rhymes which he sings or repeats accurately?

### Age 5
Does he:

❑ speak fluently, with correct grammar?

❑ pronounce most letter sounds correctly?

❑ give his full name, address, age and, sometimes, his birthday?

❑ love to sing rhymes and songs?

❑ enjoy jokes and riddles?

❑ enjoy being read to and often act out stories through play afterwards (either independently or with friends)?

❑ ask the meaning of difficult words and enjoy using them - often out of context?

# Reading and writing activities

**There are many ways in which you can help your child to make a start with these important skills.**

## READING

Words are all around us. Point them out to your child and read them together. Look at:

- posters
- addresses
- timetables
- supermarket signs
- shop names
- adverts
- maps
- road signs
- street names
- lists
- food packets
- letters and postcards

### Set an example

Let your child see you enjoying reading and making use of it in everyday life. Read:

- ❑ books (fiction and non-fiction)
- ❑ newspapers
- ❑ instructions
- ❑ letters
- ❑ labels
- ❑ lists

### Choosing books

- ❑ Make regular visits to the library.
- ❑ Select some books yourself but let your child make the selection sometimes.
- ❑ Don't choose a book on the basis of its cover - look carefully at the contents.
- ❑ Choose books with good illustrations.
- ❑ Choose books that are well written and that can be read aloud effectively.
- ❑ Choose a variety of subjects: fiction and non-fiction.
- ❑ Look at the length of a story. If it is too long, it may not hold the child's attention through to the end. Avoid books with chapters at this age.
- ❑ Look carefully at the language used. Is it within your child's understanding? Is there a variety of descriptive language...gentle words, exciting words, happy and sad passages?

- ❑ Look at the message of the story. Does it reflect the sort of attitude you want your child to adopt?
- ❑ Try writing a story for your child.

### Pre-reading games

Before your child is ready to read, it is important that she is given opportunities to look carefully at things and notice differences. The following activities will help:

- ❑ *Hunt the thimble* Your child hunts for an item hidden in the room. You can say whether she is warm or cold.

- ❑ *Spot the change* Re-position an object in the room or add another object to see if she will notice it.

- ❑ *Memory tray* Place a few items on a tray. Let your child look at it for about one minute. Cover the tray with a cloth and ask her to try to remember what she saw. Make this more difficult by adding more items.

- ❑ *What's the difference?* Draw 2 pictures with slight differences between them. Your child has to say what is different.

- ❑ *Snap* Use snap cards, or parts of 2 packs of playing cards. Your child has to match 2 cards which look the same.

- ❑ *Through the keyhole* Cut out a large keyhole shape in a large sheet of paper or card. Place it over a picture so that only part of it can be seen through the keyhole. Your child then guesses what the rest of the picture shows.

- ❑ *Letter match* Draw lower case letters (not capitals) on some envelopes and put matching badges or stickers on some of your child's toys. See if she can match the letters on the envelopes to the letters on the toys.

- ❑ *Jigsaw puzzles* You can buy jigsaws or make your own. Photocopy shops will enlarge photographs to A4 size; stick these on to card and cut them into pieces. Your child will enjoy doing jigsaw puzzles which show pictures of herself!

## Is my child ready to start reading?

Children vary enormously in this, but if your child can do most of the following, she is ready to start reading. You will encourage her if you keep an open mind, praise success and treat failure kindly.

---

### CHECKLIST

Can she:

- ❑ see and hear properly?
- ❑ pronounce words clearly?
- ❑ speak in complete sentences?
- ❑ listen to rhymes, songs and stories with enjoyment?
- ❑ understand and follow simple instructions?
- ❑ do simple games which involve recognition of shape, size and order?

---

Don't worry if your child isn't interested in reading before she starts school. Children are individuals and are ready to read at different stages.

### How do I introduce reading?

- ❑ Give your child a bookshelf (at child height) or a book box of her own.
- ❑ Introduce your child's name in writing. Explain that this collection of shapes is a word that says her name.
- ❑ Write your child's name on all her drawings and ask her what they are about. Write simple captions under the pictures (in lower case letters). Display her work carefully on the wall so that she can read the captions with you from time to time.
- ❑ Make a book using family photographs and write one-line captions to go with them.
- ❑ When reading stories to your child, point out some individual words to her.
- ❑ Buy a workbook to work through together. (See page 21 for details of workbooks published by Hodder.)
- ❑ Look out for computer programs which help beginners with spelling.

## WRITING

### Is my child ready to write?

If she is ready to read, she is probably ready to learn to write.

- ❑ Encourage pencil control by providing tracing, colouring, drawing and dot-to-dot activities.
- ❑ Teach your child how to hold a pencil correctly. A pencil grip will help her learn the correct position.
- ❑ Draw simple patterns in a pale colour for your child to trace over.
- ❑ Write simple words (lower case letters) under pictures for your child to trace over and, later, to copy underneath.
- ❑ Encourage the correct formation of letters without being critical. Always start at the top of each letter.
- ❑ Teach your child to write her own name.
- ❑ Buy a workbook to work through together. (See page 21 for details of workbooks published by Hodder.)
- ❑ Encourage your child to 'write' her own book. Provide a notebook in which she can draw pictures. Write the captions together.
- ❑ Encourage your child to write simple letters to friends and relatives and involve her in your own informal letter and greeting card writing.
- ❑ When setting the table, help your child to make place cards for each member of the family and visiting friends/relatives.

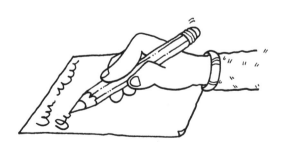

# Mathematics activities

**Numbers, like letters, provide lots of entertainment for small children. You can help your child to become familiar with the sound of number names, to begin to understand what they represent and finally to learn to recognise them when he sees them written down.**

Learning to count and learning the names of the numbers need lots of repetition, and number games are the best way to make this repetition interesting:

❏ Sing number songs and rhymes (see page 16 - Songs and music making).

❏ Point out numbers on clocks, telephones, bathroom scales, price labels etc. This helps to show that numbers are useful and that they have a purpose.

❏ As you count objects together, touch each one to show your child that he is counting one object at a time.

❏ Do not go beyond the number 3 until your child has really understood numbers 1 to 3 and can count easily, and then introduce each subsequent number one by one.

❏ Use every opportunity to count - the stairs up to bed, the spoons for the table etc.

When your child starts school, he will begin practical mathematics activities immediately. These will give him experience in using and applying mathematics by working in these areas:

> **Number**
> **Shape and space**
> **Measures**

Generally, your child needs to learn:

❏ to use mathematical language about shape, size and quantity

❏ to create patterns

❏ to compare and count objects

You can prepare him with the following activities:

## NUMBER

❏ *Picture dominoes*

❏ *Picture/number lotto*

❏ *Number dominoes* (from about age 4)

❏ *Ludo*

❏ *Dot-to-dot activities*

❏ *A counting tray* Take an egg carton or tape margarine tubs together. Write the numbers 1 to 6 on slips of paper to fit inside each compartment. Teach your child how to count the correct number of counters or buttons into each compartment.

❏ *Step, hop and jump* Give instructions such as 'Take 1 step and 2 jumps'.

❏ *Throwing games* Your child has to throw the correct number of objects into a bucket or large box.

❏ *Dice games* Draw a simple track and use buttons for counters. After the die has been thrown, your child moves a button forward the correct number of spaces.

❏ *Spinners* Cut a hexagon from card, mark the numbers 1 to 6 on the outside edges (one number for each straight edge) and push a matchstick through the centre. Use the spinner instead of a die.

❏ *Number cards* Cut out 6 postcard-sized cards. Using one card for each number from 1 to 6, write the number on one side of each card and draw and colour the corresponding number of large dots on the other side. Lay the cards out with the spots showing and ask your child to put them in order from 1 to 6.

  Make several cards for each number and arrange the spots differently so that your child can try to match the cards that have the same number of spots. This will help him to understand that the same number of spots or objects can be presented in many different ways and not just in one particular pattern.

- ❑ *Number snap* Show your child a number card and ask him to show you the correct number of buttons or counters.
- ❑ *Bingo* Make a bingo card with the numbers 1 to 6. Your child covers up the numbers as you call them out.
- ❑ *Talking about time* Discuss times of the day, days of the week, months of the year, seasons, notable calendar dates and special times such as birthdays.

## Shape and space

- ❑ *Sorting* Sort toys or the contents of a cupboard into sets, for example a set of tins and a set of packets. Cut out pictures from magazines and catalogues and sort these. Work towards encouraging your child to sort objects according to colour, shape and size.
- ❑ *2-D and 3-D shapes* Look for examples of 2-D shapes (squares, rectangles, circles, triangles) and 3-D shapes (cubes, cuboids, pyramids, spheres and cylinders). Play 'I spy' to see how many you can find, concentrating on one shape at a time. Look especially for 3-D shapes when out shopping.

## MEASURES

- ❑ *Comparisons* Help your child with the language of maths by collecting different-sized containers to use in sand and water play. Discuss which holds more and which holds less. Make comparisons between larger/smaller, heavier/lighter, longer/shorter.
- ❑ *A height and weight chart* Use this not only as a record of your child's growth and progress, but also as a way of involving him in the recording of the information.
- ❑ *Measuring* Ask questions such as 'How many cars will go along the edge of the table?' 'How many bricks tall is teddy?'

---

### Writing numbers

- ❑ All numbers (and letters) start from the top.
- ❑ Practise one number at a time.
- ❑ Draw the number for your child to trace over with a crayon or pencil.
- ❑ Draw dotted numbers for him to draw over, indicating with a large dot the point where he should start.
- ❑ Try to link the numeral and the quantity.
- ❑ Make the numbers together with playdough.
- ❑ Teach your child to write the numbers in the sand tray with his finger.

# Science activities

At the pre-school stage, science activities should be based on the child's experience of the world in the course of play or when out walking. Encourage exploration, observation and discussion of what your child sees.

The science work your child will be doing in school will be divided into these main areas:

**Life processes and living things**

**Materials and their properties**

**Physical processes**

## LIFE PROCESSES AND LIVING THINGS

This is about humans, plants and animals.

The following activities will encourage your child to be interested in living things:

❏ Talk about differences between yourself and your child, between your child and her grandparents, and between your child and her friends.

❏ Keep simple records of weight and height to show changes over time.

❏ Talk about foods which are good for us, and those which are not so good.

❏ Discuss the need for restful sleep and good exercise.

❏ Visit a farm, a safari park or a zoo to see a variety of animal life. Talk about where the animals live and what they eat. Discuss similarities and differences amongst animals.

❏ Try growing a variety of plants in the garden or in pots and discuss what the plants need in order to grow. Try growing plants in different places, with or without soil, light or heat. Make a bottle garden together.

❏ Explain how plants and pet animals need proper care to keep them healthy.

❏ Encourage your child to care for the environment.

## MATERIALS AND THEIR PROPERTIES

This is about how materials differ and how some are able to do things that others cannot.

The following activities will help your child to start investigating materials:

❏ Collect lots of different materials, both natural and synthetic. Talk about how they feel. Think about words to describe them, such as 'hard', 'soft', 'shiny', 'rough', 'smooth'. Experiment to see whether the materials bend or stretch.

❏ Play games where your child has to select a material which fits the description you give.

❏ Look at the way some materials let the light shine through them while others do not.

❏ Overlap coloured tissue or cellophane and let your child look through it.

❏ Mix paints together to see what happens.

❏ Encourage your child to draw with wax crayons and see what happens when she paints over the top with water paints.

❏ Let your child mix ingredients when you are following a recipe. Point out the changes brought about by heating things or putting them in the freezer.

❏ On winter days, bring in some snow or ice to see what happens to it.

## PHYSICAL PROCESSES

This is about forces, light, energy and sounds.

- ❑ Show the difference between pushes and pulls. See if your child can identify whether she is pushing or pulling.

- ❑ Let your child sort some toys into those which she pulls and those which she pushes.

- ❑ Roll toy cars down a gentle slope, and then increase the angle of the slope. What do you notice?

- ❑ Compare pushing toys on a rough surface with pushing toys on a smooth surface.

- ❑ Talk about moving air (wind). Fly a kite, or look at washing on a washing line. Compare how it moves in a strong wind and in a gentle breeze. What are the signs of moving air? Look at leaves, smoke, clouds, litter and trees.

- ❑ When your child is playing with water, test to see which things float or sink.

- ❑ Make a water jet with a washing-up liquid bottle. Test to see if it can move things.

- ❑ Make a collection of magnets. Test to see which materials are attracted.

- ❑ Look at shadows and see how they are made. Are they always the same? Are they always in the same place? On a sunny day, go outside and have fun playing shadow games. Make wide shapes, narrow shapes, tall and short shapes. Look at shadows made by different objects.

- ❑ Keep a simple record of the weather and the seasons. Encourage your child to observe differences between the seasons. Link these observations to the clothes that we wear, or to special events at different times of the year.

- ❑ Listen to a variety of sounds. Discuss whether they are loud or soft sounds. Make a tape recording of different sounds and see if your child can identify them.

- ❑ Investigate striking, plucking and shaking. Look at a variety of instruments to see how sounds are made.

Make all the activities fun! Adopt a 'let's find out together' approach and encourage your child to be a science detective, always on the look-out for clues to answer the question 'Why?'

# Songs and music making

You don't need to play an instrument or have a wonderful singing voice to introduce a pre-school child to music. All you need is the enthusiasm to teach your child a few rhymes or songs and to introduce him to rhythm in an entertaining way. Through learning the rhymes your child will develop his vocabulary and his listening skills. The introduction of clapping or percussion instruments will help to develop his sense of rhythm.

These activities will encourage your child to take an interest in music making:

❑ Play lots of different music at home.

❑ Sing to and with your child as a normal part of your day - in the bath, or when getting dressed or out for a walk.

❑ Introduce new rhymes and songs gradually and keep returning to the ones which are most familiar to your child.

❑ Sing along to nursery rhyme and song tapes.

❑ Use visual aids - pictures, toys, puppets - to maintain concentration and give greater meaning and impact to the song.

❑ Encourage your child to experiment with both loud and quiet singing.

❑ Teach him how to clap to music.

❑ Make music: rattle railings, clash pan lids, chime milk bottles.

❑ Play musical games - ask your child to hum a tune for you to guess what it is.

❑ Dance together - to any music you like!

❑ Play games where your child moves to music and changes his movements to suit the mood.

❑ Find out about children's television and radio programmes with a music-making element.

❑ Find out about local music lessons, such as group singing and simple percussion.

Make all the activities fun, and don't expect too much too soon.

## INTRODUCING PERCUSSION

Percussion instruments include:

- bells
- maracas
- finger cymbals
- castanets
- triangles
- tambourines
- drums
- small wood blocks etc.

❑ Help your child to make his own music with home-made instruments - dried peas in a plastic pot, or a wooden spoon on a tin.

❑ Remember that any instruments that you introduce, whether bought or home-made, should be safe, sound appealing, look attractive and be stored in a special box - which your child could decorate.

❑ Keep things simple - use only one percussion instrument for each song.

❑ Select instruments according to the song or rhyme being sung: for example, a castanet works well with the quacking sounds in 'Five little ducks', as do bells accompanying 'Mary, Mary, quite contrary'.

❑ Initially, just encourage your child to play the percussion instrument as you sing the song. This should encourage him to concentrate on the rhythm. As he gains confidence he may want to sing along as well as play an instrument.

# SONGS AND RHYMES TO SING TOGETHER

## Counting rhymes

Five little ducks

Five currant buns

Five fat sausages

Five little speckled frogs

One, two, buckle my shoe

One, two, three, four, five,
(once I caught a fish alive)

Peter hammers with one hammer

### Finger rhymes

Hickory, dickory, dock

Tommy Thumb

Incy-Wincy Spider

Two fat gentlemen met in a lane

Two little dicky-birds

## Singing and dancing songs

In and out the dusty bluebells

London Bridge is falling down

Oranges and lemons

Ring-a-ring o'roses

The farmer's in his den

The grand old Duke of York

The Hokey Cokey

## Action songs

Head, shoulders, knees and toes

Here we go round the mulberry bush

I'm a little teapot

I hear thunder

Row, row, row your boat

See the little bunny sleeping

When all the cows were sleeping

Wind the bobbin up

Michael Finnigin

Miss Polly had a dolly

Old MacDonald had a farm

The wheels on the bus

Old John Muddlecombe

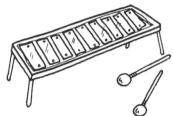

## Traditional nursery rhymes

Hey, diddle, diddle

Humpty Dumpty

Jack and Jill

Little Boy Blue

Little Miss Muffet

Mary had a little lamb

Mary, Mary, quite contrary

There was a crooked man

Twinkle, twinkle, little star

# Art and craft

Through art and craft activities your child will learn to explore colour, texture, shape and space. She will learn to express ideas and feelings in a variety of ways whilst exploring a variety of materials. She will find the results satisfying and will build upon a wide range of skills in the process.

You can help by:

❏ providing a variety of materials:

- wax crayons
- crayons
- chalks
- mixing palettes
- crepe paper
- newspaper
- cellophane
- playdough
- safety scissors
- glue
- felt-tipped pens (washable)
- scraps of material for collage
- pencils
- paints
- sugar paper
- tissue paper
- aluminium foil
- tracing paper
- card
- clay
- junk materials
- a variety of brushes and sponges
- sticky paper squares in various colours

❏ making sure that the materials your child can safely handle alone are easily accessible for her to pick up when she wants to

❏ providing protective clothing for your child and covering all surfaces so that she can enjoy being creative without feeling anxious

❏ showing your child how to experiment with paints to create different textures and effects; try adding washing-up liquid, PVA glue or icing sugar and look carefully at the results

❏ giving your child lots of opportunities to experiment

❏ collecting natural objects for collage when out walking together (seeds, twigs, bark, feathers, stones, pebbles, shells, grasses)

❏ letting her draw and scribble and showing her how to draw if she asks

❏ encouraging her to talk about her picture and how she feels about it

❏ never rushing your child to finish a piece of work

❏ not expecting works of art, but giving your child the opportunity to make discoveries about the materials being used and to express herself through them

❏ showing interest and appreciation and treating your child's work with care and respect

❏ finding a book with creative ideas for your child's age group

❏ displaying special pieces of work, to encourage a sense of pride in the achievement

## ACTIVITIES USING PAINT

❏ **Finger painting** Use thick paint such as poster paint in a shallow container. Alternatively, use powder paint mixed with wallpaper paste. Make prints on sugar paper.

❏ **Blot painting** Drop blots of thin paint on to paper. Fold the paper and press out the blots to make the paint travel. Open to see the results.

❏ **Blowing paint** Put a large drop of thin paint on to paper and blow through a thick straw to make the paint travel.

❏ **Bubble painting** Mix a little washing-up liquid with a small amount of powder paint and water. Blow into the mixture with a thick straw to create coloured bubbles. Place paper gently over the top of the bubbles, trying not to burst them. You could repeat this using a different coloured mixture, and make a bubble print on top of the first one.

❏ **Potato/sponge/leaf printing** Cut out sponge shapes or cut potatoes in half. Make up thick paint solutions in various colours and put them in shallow containers. Show your child how to dip the sponge/potato/leaf into the paint and then press it on the paper.

You could try cutting a shape into a potato.

> DON'T ALLOW YOUR CHILD TO DO THIS.

❏ **Wax-resist pictures** Draw a picture or pattern in wax crayon and paint over it with a water-based paint.

### Recipe for playdough
(to be made by an adult)

1 cup salt

2 cups flour

4 teaspoons cream of tartar

2 tablespoons cooking oil

2 cups water

powder paint or food colouring

Mix the ingredients in a saucepan. Add the paint/colouring. Cook on medium heat for 3 – 5 minutes, stirring until the mixture becomes stiff. Store in an airtight container in the refrigerator.

## OTHER ACTIVITIES

❏ Collage

❏ Junk modelling

❏ Papier mâché

❏ Kite making

❏ Puppet making

❏ Mask making

❏ Clay/playdough modelling

# Resources for learning

Television, video, radio, audio tapes and computers are all very valuable sources of entertainment and learning. The following are general guidelines for their effective use.

## TELEVISION AND VIDEO

❏ Encourage your child to be selective and make choices about what he watches. Look through the television guides together and if possible watch the programme yourself before your child sees it.

❏ Be with your child as often as possible while he is watching. Talk about the programme and be ready to answer questions.

❏ Have a set time for watching and encourage him to ask whether he can watch television.

❏ Remember that play and physical exercise should not be overlooked.

❏ If you wish, you could show your child how to switch on the television and load and operate the video recorder. Safety is very important so you must decide whether or not to teach this skill.

❏ Let your child choose a programme or video for himself sometimes. Encourage him to say why he chose it.

❏ Provide a variety of video tapes: cartoons, stories, action rhymes, wildlife and natural history programmes. In particular, look out for early years and schools' broadcasts.

❏ Watch home learning videos. Many are presented by popular children's characters.

❏ Use your own video camera or stills camera to make your own programmes or to record an event. Your child could provide the commentary.

## RADIO AND AUDIO TAPES

These encourage children to use their imagination far more than when watching television, and they help to develop listening skills and concentration.

❏ Listen to schools' and children's programmes on the radio.

❏ Set aside some time each week for listening to story tapes and make a comfortable corner where you can listen together.

❏ Provide a robust, battery-operated tape recorder that is simple to load and operate. Your child can then listen when he wants to. The addition of headphones may encourage greater concentration and add to the novelty.

❏ Build up a library of story tapes and books. Many give a signal during the story to indicate when to turn the page. Try making your own story tapes to accompany favourite books.

❏ Sit with your child as often as possible and follow the words together. This conveys the idea that print carries meaning.

❏ Talk about the stories afterwards. Discuss favourite parts and characters.

## COMPUTERS

❏ As with television and video, children should not spend too much time playing computer games. Set time limits and be ready to offer alternative forms of amusement.

❏ Sit with your child and show him how to switch on and load the system. Introduce the functions of the various keys at a pace he can cope with.

❏ Build confidence with lots of repetition and encourage your child to handle the keys gently. Be there to help with difficulties and remember that we all learn by making mistakes.

❏ Be selective about software - many computer games are only for fun and most only encourage quick reaction. Ask the headteacher of the school your child will be going to which kind of computer and software they recommend. When buying software, you can ask for a demonstration before you make a decision.

❏ Try computer games and battery-operated machines to help with simple adding or spelling.

❏ Look at some of the interactive books on CD-ROM; these provide excellent opportunities for shared learning at any age. You will need to check that your computer is suitable for CD-ROM.

## WORKBOOKS

The Hodder Home Learning series has been designed to prepare children and their parents for the formal skills that they will encounter in school. The books in this series which are suitable for 3 to 5 year-olds include: *Reading*, *Writing*, *Numbers*, *Reading Practice*, *Writing Practice* and *Number Practice*. Each has been prepared in consultation with teachers and educationists, and all are supported by the National Confederation of Parent Teacher Associations (NCPTA). The series forms an ideal platform for discussion about school.

The workbooks in this series should be used to encourage:

❏ discussion

❏ a home learning routine

❏ problem-solving skills

❏ concentration and the ability to complete a task

❏ an enjoyment of learning

❏ an interest in a variety of subjects

❏ a sense of achievement and confidence, which in turn can lead to success

Once your child has completed the books in the 3 to 5 age band there are a further 3 age bands to support him throughout all his primary years. These may be used to provide extra help with a subject or to develop a particular interest.

# Choosing a playgroup or nursery

In the playgroup or nursery your child will meet other children and form friendships. She will also meet other adults who will, for a time, replace you in a guidance role. A good pre-school education is tailored to the needs of the very young and positively helps growth.

*What's the difference between a nursery and a playgroup?*

Playgroups are voluntary groups, usually non-profit-making, and nurseries are usually run by a private company or the local authority and staffed by professionals.

| | PLAYGROUPS | NURSERIES |
|---|---|---|
| **Who runs them?** | Most playgroups are affiliated to the Pre-school Playgroups Association. The PPA aims to 'provide safe and satisfying group play in which parents have a right to take part. It promotes community situations where parents can work together to meet some of the growing needs of young children'.<br><br>Playgroups are usually run by parents of young children or those whose children have been to the playgroup. The PPA provides training for play leaders, monitors playgroups and provides guidance. The local authority monitors playgroups in its area. | *Day nurseries* are usually staffed by qualified nursery nurses. They are either privately run or run by the local authority. *State nursery schools* are staffed by qualified teachers and nursery nurses. The emphasis is on working together. *Private nursery schools* Staff do not need formal educational qualifications. *Montessori nursery schools* are privately run but staff are trained in the 'Montessori' teaching method and philosophy. These nurseries focus on individual development, encouraging self-reliance and motivation. |
| **Are they in special premises?** | Not always - they usually share a community building such as a church hall. There may be no special facilities such as small toilets and washbasins. | Nurseries are usually purpose-built or specially refurbished internally. Many state nursery schools are attached to primary schools. Nurseries have child-centred fittings such as low handles and pegs and small toilets. |
| **What equipment do they have?** | They have their own toys and learning equipment which are set out by the play leaders before each session. They usually have small tables and chairs too. | Nurseries have a full range of play/learning equipment, often with special outdoor play areas. Montessori nurseries usually have special equipment that links in with the teaching method. |
| **How old are the children, and how long do they stay?** | Most of the children are 3 to 5 years old. Most go for 1 year before they start school, but some go for 2 years. | *Day nurseries* - 0 to 5 year-olds; variable *Nursery schools* - 3 to 5 year-olds; usually 1 year. |
| **How many children can go?** | There are usually 8 children to 1 adult, and no fewer than 2 adults. | *Day care* - 1 adult to 5 children aged 2+ - 1 adult to 4 children aged below 2 *Sessional care* - 1 adult to 8 children aged 2+ - 1 adult to 4 children aged below 2 - 1 adult to 5 children if majority are aged 2+ |

| | PLAYGROUPS | NURSERIES |
|---|---|---|
| **How long are the sessions?** | Most groups offer 2 sessions a week only - they usually have a waiting list. Sessions may be morning or afternoon to fit in with older siblings at school. | *Day nurseries* – by arrangement<br>*State nursery schools* – morning or afternoon<br>*Private nursery schools* – by arrangement |
| **What's the cost?** | Costs vary: £1-£2.50 per session is about average. | *State nurseries* are free.<br>*Private nurseries* vary in cost. |
| **Does my child need any special skills?** | She must be toilet-trained and confident enough to leave you, though many playgroups will help your child gain confidence by letting you stay for a while to begin with. | Check with individual nurseries. |
| **What do the children do?** | They do not usually do any 'formal' school work – the emphasis is on development through play and social learning:<br><br>❑ large play apparatus: slides, indoor climbing frames, trampolines, play houses<br>❑ small play equipment: jigsaws, construction toys<br>❑ art and craft work: cutting, sticking, painting, model making<br>❑ baking<br>❑ free play: toy bicycles/tricycles and cars<br>❑ quiet times listening to a story<br>❑ singing and games with songs<br>❑ snack time, lining up and taking turns | The activities are much the same as at playgroup except for specialist nurseries such as Montessori. State nurseries may have a more formal approach and introduce writing and number and 'school' behaviour. |
| **Do they encourage parental involvement?** | Parents are encouraged to help on a rota basis under the guidance of the play leaders. Parents can join the committee who run the group, making policy decisions and fundraising. | There is very little parental involvement – considerably less than at a playgroup. State nurseries sometimes have parents helping. |
| **Are there local authority guidelines?** | ❑ A clean, light room with safe fires and heaters<br>❑ A fire exit and opening windows<br>❑ All equipment and furniture to be in good order<br>❑ A first-aid box and a person trained in first aid<br>❑ Toilet facilities (1 toilet to 10 children)<br>❑ Clean kitchen facilities for mid-session snack<br>❑ No smoking while working with children<br>❑ Daily register, and a record of home addresses and contact phone numbers<br>❑ Safely fenced, outdoor play space with adult supervision | The same conditions apply as for playgroups. |

# Choosing a school

It is never too soon to start looking at the various schools available to your child to find the one that you think would best suit his needs. Don't wait until he is nearly of school age as you may find that there is a shortage of places.

## FIRST STEPS

❑ Consult people who have experience of the schools available. Ask neighbours, parents at playgroup, teachers and your children's friends.

❑ Phone the local education authority and ask for their list of local primary schools.

❑ Look in the telephone directory for lists of private schools. Many local papers run a page of advertisements once a year.

### Practical considerations

The proximity of school to home can be a consideration but other factors may be more important.

❑ Is it safe or feasible to walk to the school, or is transport necessary?

❑ Local friends may go to the same school and consequently may play together after school too.

❑ If your child is sick or has an accident during school hours, you may need to be able to get there quickly.

❑ You may want to feel part of the community.

❑ You may want to choose a school near your place of work, or your partner's.

## MAKING A START

❑ Phone the headteachers of a few schools and ask if places are available.

❑ Make an appointment to look round during school hours.

❑ The following is a list of things you might want to look out for when visiting a school. (If you don't want to take a list, consider things under the headings: People, Curriculum, Equipment, Building).

• Does the entrance hall seem welcoming? Are there any interesting displays?

• Do the children talk easily with the teachers?

• Are the children polite and relatively quiet?

• How are you treated by the teachers and the children?

• What information are you given?

• Does the school have a religious bias?

• How many children are there in the school and in each class?

• What sort of ancillary help is there (classroom assistants, volunteers, parents)?

• Is there any special provision for disabled children, children with learning difficulties or very bright children?

• How do the children behave in the playground or when moving around the school?

• How are the children supervised at playtime and lunch-time, and before and after school?

• What are the security arrangements?

• Is there a lot of the children's own work on the walls?

• Can you see examples of work in maths, English, science, art, music, technology, computers and physical education?

• What sort of equipment can you see? Look out for computers, large P E equipment, play areas and a well stocked library containing a variety of books.

- Is the building well maintained, tidy and clean?

- What is the playground like? Are there gardens or a field? Is there a special playground for the youngest children?

- Does the school follow a particular reading or maths scheme?

- What sort of records are kept about the children? Do parents have an opportunity to see them?

- What does the school do in the case of accident or illness?

- Is there a PTA (Parent Teacher Association)? What does it do?

- Is there a happy, productive atmosphere?

- Do you like the school?

# The National Curriculum

The National Curriculum describes a set of subjects which must be taught in all state schools in England and Wales. Each subject has been clearly laid out in a detailed document that outlines all the knowledge and skills to be taught at each stage. The National Curriculum is based on a system of assessment by which the teacher monitors the progress of all the individuals in her class.

## WHO DESIGNED THE NATIONAL CURRICULUM?

The Government designed it in consultation with teachers and other educational experts, and the teachers in schools make sure that it works for the children.

## DOES THE NATIONAL CURRICULUM CHANGE?

Yes, it has been changed many times since it was first introduced. Many of these changes have been recommended by teachers who have used the National Curriculum in schools. There are no more changes planned for the near future.

## DO PRIVATE SCHOOLS HAVE TO TEACH THE NATIONAL CURRICULUM?

No, it is compulsory in state schools only, but many private schools choose to use it.

## IS THE NATIONAL CURRICULUM ALL THAT IS TAUGHT IN SCHOOLS?

The National Curriculum is the framework, but much more goes on in schools. The school prospectus will give you this information.

## WHICH SUBJECTS ARE TAUGHT IN THE NATIONAL CURRICULUM?

Primary schools (children from 4-11 years old) concentrate on 3 Core subjects:

| Mathematics | English | Science |
|---|---|---|

There are 6 other subjects (Foundation subjects) which broaden knowledge but have to be given less time:

| Technology | Art | Music |
|---|---|---|
| History | Geography | PE |

**Welsh** is taught in Wales – as a Core subject in Welsh-speaking schools and as a Foundation subject in other schools.

## WHAT ABOUT RELIGION?

All children take RE unless their parents choose otherwise. Ask about your local education authority's policy.

## WHAT IS TAUGHT IN EACH SUBJECT?

Each subject is divided into areas of learning called Attainment Targets (ATs) and the children are given experience of each area.

### Mathematics

*AT1 Using and applying mathematics*

*AT2 Number*

*AT3 Shape, space and measures*

*AT4 Handling data*
*(only for Key Stage 2 – juniors )*

### English

*AT1 Speaking and listening*

*AT2 Reading*

*AT3 Writing:* • *composition*
  • *punctuation*
  • *spelling*
  • *handwriting*

### Science

*AT1 Experimental and investigative science*

*AT2 Life processes and living things*

*AT3 Materials and their properties*

*AT4 Physical processes*

Information for each of the subjects is presented in its own ring-binder. Parents can see these documents at school or buy their own copies from:

HMSO Publications Centre
PO Box 276
London SW8 5DT
Tel: 0171 873 9090

## HOW DOES THE NATIONAL CURRICULUM AFFECT THE INFANT CLASSES?

Infant children start working with the National Curriculum at Key Stage 1. Key Stage 1 includes the reception class and Years 1 and 2, to make 3 infant years. In their final infant year (Year 2) children do their first National Curriculum Standard Assessment Tasks (SATs) when most are 7 years old.

## WHAT COMES AFTER THE INFANT YEARS (KEY STAGE 1)?

The junior stage is called Key Stage 2 which lasts for 4 years. The classes are called Years 3, 4, 5 and 6. In Year 6, when most children are 11, further SATs are given. Secondary schools cater for Key Stages 3 and 4, with additional SATs given to 14 and 16 year-olds.

## WHAT ARE THE STANDARD ASSESSMENT TASKS?

These are a series of national assessments designed to help teachers assess how well individual children are developing compared to others in the same age group. The aim is that the children should see them not as tests, but rather as a continuation of the topics they study on a daily basis. Parents see the results in the school report and will usually have opportunities to discuss the results with the class teacher.

### Remember

Each child is an individual.

Children develop at different rates in different subjects.

The National Curriculum is designed to take account of this and to help your child to progress.

# Preparing for school

If your child can do the following things before he starts school, many problems can be avoided. Give him plenty of support as he learns and provide plenty of contact with other children and adults.

❑ *Get dressed and undressed independently* Choose clothes that your child can manage by himself and give lots of practice with zips and buttons.

❑ *Put on his own shoes* Teach your child to put his shoes on the correct feet and to tie his shoelaces.

❑ *Put on his coat and gloves* Your child may find mittens easier than gloves. Attach mittens or gloves to a length of yarn to prevent them from getting lost.

❑ *Recognise his own things* Mark your child's name on all his possessions. You can buy name tapes to sew or iron on to clothes.

❑ *Use the toilet independently and wash his hands afterwards*

❑ *Eat lunch independently* Teach your child how to use a knife and fork (especially if he will be having a school lunch); if your child will be having a packed lunch, make sure he knows how to open his lunch box and his drink container.

❑ *Make decisions* Your child will need to get used to making choices at school, from choosing an activity or partner to deciding what to eat at lunch-time. Give him lots of experience of making everyday decisions at home beforehand.

❑ *Ask for help* Your child should have the confidence to ask for help when he needs it. Encourage him to speak up for himself – at playgroup, in the local shop or with friends and relatives. Build up his confidence gradually.

If your child has any special medical needs or requirements such as a hearing aid or an asthma inhaler, let the teacher know and ask whether there is someone to take responsibility for any equipment or medicine. If your child wears glasses, make sure the teacher knows whether they should be worn all the time or just occasionally.

## PUTTING YOUR CHILD'S NAME DOWN FOR SCHOOL

❑ Take your child's birth certificate to the school with you.

❑ The school will advise you of:
- pre-school events
- the class your child will be joining and the teacher's name
- any equipment or clothes he might need
- information about lunches
- a list of holidays and starting dates
- any pre-school tasks you can do

# PREPARING FOR THE FIRST DAY

❑ Don't make too much fuss or build up your child's hopes too high, but do encourage him to look forward to the event.

❑ Visit the school with your child as much as possible beforehand to make it familiar.

❑ Let your child meet other children who go to the school.

❑ Go to school fairs and sports days together.

❑ Look through the school fence together at playtimes to see the children playing.

❑ Make sure your child knows the names of his new teacher, the nursery nurse and the headteacher.

❑ Buy a story book about starting school.

❑ Make sure your child knows where the toilets are and where to hang his coat.

❑ Tell him where you will meet him at home time and make every effort not to be late! Most reception teachers make sure all the children have been collected.

### Remember

❑ Most children enjoy the first day at school but think that there's no need to go again!

❑ Many seem independent but get exhausted after a few weeks of a new routine.

❑ Don't do too many after-school activities during the first term – your child may be too tired the next day.

❑ Be understanding, supportive and encouraging.

❑ Most children enjoy school and look forward to it!

# Getting involved with school

Most primary schools welcome and rely on help from parents. You can help in a variety of ways depending on your talents and work commitments.

## WHAT SORT OF HELP IS NEEDED?

❑ Helping small groups of children with tasks such as baking, artwork, computer work and reading

❑ Practical jobs around the school such as gardening, sorting out the library or store-room or renovating equipment

❑ Helping with the setting up and running of school events such as fairs, jumble sales, sports days, dances and parties

❑ Accompanying groups of children on school outings or providing lifts to events away from school

## SHOULD I OFFER ANY SPECIAL SKILLS OR TALENTS?

❑ There are many jobs that are of great interest to children. For instance, do you work for the police, fire, ambulance or medical services? Could you talk to children about your work?

❑ Do you have a talent: musical, artistic, sporty, technical or practical?

## WHAT QUALITIES DO I NEED?

❑ Willingness to help with anything
❑ Kindness
❑ Discretion
❑ Commitment

## HOW SHOULD I BEHAVE IN THE CLASSROOM?

❑ Follow the teacher's lead, especially in matters of discipline.

❑ Try to help everyone in your charge without bias.

❑ Listen to what the children say.

❑ Be discreet if you hear personal details.

❑ Offer help if you see a need.

## JOINING A PARENTS' GROUP

Most schools recognise the important contribution that parents can make to the school and are keen to support parents' efforts.

A home/school group may be called any of the following: PTA (Parent Teacher Association), Parents' Association, Friends of ... or Home School Association (HSA). These groups are linked nationally through the NCPTA (National Confederation of Parent Teacher Associations) which brings together over 10,500 Home School Associations and represents 6 million parents and children. These groups:

❑ encourage parents to get involved with school life, leading to a greater sense of belonging and a better understanding about what is happening in school

❑ provide opportunities for parents to meet other parents

❑ encourage parents and teachers to talk in an informal atmosphere, enabling parents to feel at ease within the school environment

❑ promote community spirit through social events involving parents, teachers and children

❑ raise money for the school; although fundraising is not the most important function of a Home School Association, schools are always extremely appreciative of financial help, and fundraising is fun and a good opportunity to work as a team

The Home School Association runs conferences for its members. For more information about the HSA, write to:

NCPTA
2 Ebbsfleet Estate
Stonebridge Road
Gravesend
Kent
DA11 9DZ

For information about parents' rights, ask at your local library for the pamphlet 'Parents' Charter'.

# When help is needed

There are many factors in a child's life that may affect learning. If you are concerned that your child may be experiencing difficulties, try talking to family and friends in the first instance. They know you and your child best and may be able to offer advice. If you are still concerned, consider the following areas of help and the organisations listed. Please send an s.a.e. if you want them to post information to you.

## DEVELOPMENTAL ENQUIRIES

If your child appears to have difficulty with one or a number of the activities outlined in this book, some of the following people may be able to help:

- ❑ Your Health Visitor
- ❑ Your family doctor
- ❑ A nursery/school teacher
- ❑ The school clinic doctor
- ❑ An optician
- ❑ An audiologist
- ❑ A speech therapist

## YOU AND YOUR FAMILY

**Parentline**
Endway House
The Endway
Hadleigh
Essex  SS7 2AN

*A helpline for parents experiencing difficulties with children*

Tel: 01702 559900

**Advisory Centre for Education**
22 Highbury Grove
London
N5 2DQ

Tel: 0171 354 8321

**National Confederation of Parent Teacher Associations (NCPTA)**
2 Ebbsfleet Estate
Stonebridge Road
Gravesend
Kent
DA11 9DZ

Tel: 01474 560618

**Education Otherwise**
PO Box 7420
London
N99 SG

*Support and advice for those wishing to educate children at home*

Tel: 0891 518303

**Relate**
Herbert Gray College
Little Church Street
Rugby
Warwickshire
CV21 3AP

Tel: 01788 573241

**National Council for the Divorced and Separated**
PO Box 519
Leicester
LE2 3ZE

Tel: 0116 2700595

**Kidscape**
152 Buckingham Palace Road
London
SW1W 9TR

*Advice and help about safety, bullying and abuse*

Tel: 0171 730 3300

**National Children's Centre**
Brian Jackson House
New North Parade
Huddersfield
West Yorkshire
HD1 5JP

*Support and information*

Tel: 01484 519988

## MEDICAL CONDITIONS THAT AFFECT LEARNING

**British Dyslexia Association**
98 London Road
Reading
Berkshire
RG1 5AU

Tel: 01734 668271

**British Diabetic Association**
10 Queen Anne Street
London
W1M OBD

Tel: 0171 323 1531
Careline: 0171 636 6112

**British Epilepsy Association**
Anstey House
40 Hanover Square
Leeds LS3 1BE

Tel: 0113 243 9393
Helpline: 0800 30 9030

**National Asthma Campaign**
Providence House
Providence Place
London
N1 0NT

Tel: 0171 226 2260
Helpline: 0345 010203

**National Deaf Children's Society**
15 Dufferin Street
London
EC1Y 8PD

*Help, support and advice*

Tel: 0171 250 0123
Family helpline: 0800 252380

**Royal National Institute for the Blind**
224 Great Portland Street
London
W1N 6AA
Tel: 0171 388 1266

**Hyperactive Children's Support Group**
71 Whyke Lane
Chichester
West Sussex
PO19 2LD
Tel: 01903 725182

**National Association for Special Educational Needs**
NASEN House
4/5 Amber Business Village
Amber Close
Tamworth
Staffordshire
B77 4RP
Tel: 01827 311500

**Parents in Partnership**
70 South Lambeth Road
London
SW8 1RL
Tel: 0171 735 7735

## SPECIAL AREAS OF LEARNING

**National Association for Gifted Children**
Park Campus
Boughton Green Road
Northampton
NN2 7AL
Tel: 01604 792300

**Multilingual Matters**
Frankfurt Lodge
Clevedon Hall
Victoria Road
Clevedon
N Somerset
BS21 7SJ
Tel: 01275 876519

**Mensa Foundation for Gifted Children**
Mensa House
St John's Square
Wolverhampton
WV2 4AH
TeL: 01902 772771

## PLAY

**National Voluntary Council for Children's Play**
359 Euston Road
London
NW1 3AL
Tel: 0171 388 0330

**British Association for Early Childhood Education**
111 City View House
463 Bethnal Green Road
London
E2 9QY
Tel: 0171 739 7594

**Pre-school Playgroups Association**
61 Kings Cross Road
London
WC1X 9LL
Tel: 0171 833 0991
Helpline: 0171 837 5513

**National Association of Toy and Leisure Libraries**
('Play Matters')
68 Churchway
London
NW1 1LT
*Contact addresses for the loan of toys, books, tapes, games*
Tel: 0171 387 9592

## LEGAL/OFFICIAL ENQUIRIES

**NCPTA**
(see above)

**Education Otherwise**
(see above)

**Department for Education and Employment**
Sanctuary Buildings
Great Smith Street
London
SW1P 3BT
Tel: 0800 242323

**Advisory Centre for Education**
(see above)

**Citizens' Advice Bureau**
(see local telephone directory)

**Local Education Authority**
(see local telephone directory)

ISBN 0 340 67281 1

Text copyright © 1996
Jim Fitzsimmons and Rhona Whiteford

Illustrations copyright © 1996
Sascha Lipscomb

The rights of Jim Fitzsimmons and Rhona Whiteford to be identified as the authors of this work have been asserted by them in accordance with the Copyright, Design and Patents Act 1988.

First published in Great Britain 1996

10 9 8 7 6 5 4 3 2 1

Published by Hodder Children's Books, a division of Hodder Headline plc, 338 Euston Road, London NW1 3BH

Printed and bound in Great Britain

A CIP record is registered by and held at the British Library.